Here
From
Somewhere
Else

Judith Arcana

Here
From
Somewhere
Else

Left
Fork

Winner, 2015 Turtle Island Quarterly
Editor's Choice Chapbook Award

Turtle Island Quarterly sponsors
the annual Editor's Choice Chapbook Award.
Awards are chosen by the editors.
More information available at
http://fourdirectionpoetry.wix.com/turtleisland

Some of these poems were first published in the following
journals/collections, some with different titles and/or in
different versions: *Turtle Island Quarterly*, *About Place*,
Thresholds, *The Temple*, *Prairie Hearts*, *Junctures*,
Verse Wisconsin, *Passager*, *Poems and Plays*, *Bridges*,
Sugar Mule, *The Water Portfolio*, *Studio*, *Elohi Gadugi*,
and *Nimrod*.

Cover image *Composting* © Gwyn Kirk
(felted wool on silk, beads, tree coral, leaf button,
silk snips, and embroidery thread)

Cover photo by Jonathan Arlook
About the Author photo by Nancy Hill
Back cover photo by Alan Borrud

Cover design by Ryan Forsythe

ISBN-13 978-0-692-58952-6

First Left Fork Edition,
December 2015

www.LeftFork.org

This is for Jonathan.

Contents

Tom always asks the visiting poets about their influences;
this time, it's nature poets. 3

Dreaming the Indian Ocean 4

You ask me what it's like here 5

Sun from the Lake 6

Darkening Sky Above Garages 8

City River 9

The Crows 10

All That We Do Here 11

What the Birds Say 12

Soon 14

After years of graceful branches 16

This Side of the River 18

The Man Who Loves Trees 19

Birth Days 20

Here From Somewhere Else 21

Metamorphoses 22

Wild River Sister 23

Light Falling Here 24

Here
From
Somewhere
Else

Tom always asks the visiting poets about their influences; this time, it's nature poets.

I did see what might have been
a kind of kingfisher, dark blue
perched in a white March aspen
tufted head displayed in profile.
Mary Oliver was nowhere nearby.
When my sharp intake of breath
– my surprise and tiny awe –
startled the bird into flight
I thought of her, the ways
into my urban mind she had
opened, years ago. I thought
of her prayers, her questions
and of my own.

Walking the woods in deep snow
I gave myself to quiet, readily
as I'd ever given myself (not
surrender, gift). Frost's poem
– the one with the little horse –
learned when I was fifteen
given to me though he didn't
mean to, was in my mind. His
words had taken me to trees
in the snow back then, so
trees in the snow took me back
to those words. No birds.
Flown south by now.

Dreaming the Indian Ocean

You old ones, my people, when you passed childhood
were you surprised to learn so many had the same dream?
Had you thought, like me, you were the only small one
who turned your bed to a boat in the clear deep water
a boat in deep blue sky, sailing and flying the world?
Did you get where you wanted to go? Where was that?

I wanted to fly in my bed all the way to the Indian Ocean
where the great whales of every sea would swim green
deep water each year, giving birth and nursing their young.
What made that my dream? What could I have known, then
of their lives? This is the mystery left from my youth, deep
in the time before knowledge. The rest, now, I understand.

You ask me what it's like here

If I tell you —

the birds, startled up out of dry prairie grass by my footsteps

white flowers, opening themselves above dark green leaves

tunnels of black branches over muddy grass in the path

the deep sky with colors, and a tree, one tall big tree

all the crows go at sundown to that big tall tree, calling and calling

and the spring coming up small dust storms in water

— will you have it, then?

Sun from the Lake

Here, where the prairies ended
in what once was the marsh of Chicago
the sun rises out of the lake
every morning.

As light brightens the edges
of our window blinds
burning off dreams like fog –
the sun, blocks away, is rising
coral, with a nimbus of gold
surprising the gulls (who should have
been expecting it), who every night
balance webbed feet on the weathered lake pilings
or float on the dark swell of Michigan
until the water silvers in dawn, every day
lighting wilderness, there in the lake of the city.

And when the full sky lies down
on the water, covering the line of horizon
where fire breaches lake every day –
on those dark days, the sun is still rising
it rises a secret, hidden inside murky dawns
that slide through our windows all pale
(no gold to their white) so we can forget
as our dreams disappear, the wafer of fire
is rising, climbing the sky. We forget
on those days, wrapped in the veil of the city
the sun still rises behind clouds, mist, smoke.

What if we always went down to the water
all of us, there at the edge of dark water
to wait for it, mornings? What if we
went every day, every day, even in rain
when we knew it was hidden, mystery
of dawnlight, out there, behind darkness?
Then we couldn't forget (we could never
not know). It would be inside of us then.
Sun rising out of the lake every day
sunsilver burning, burning into gold –
morningfire opening our dreams.

Darkening Sky Above Garages

You must not think when dawn comes
there's no beauty in the city. Everything here
shines mirrored in towers, in sheets of light:
copper glass in flames behind the grime
of bus windows. We pass through that fire.

Do not believe there's no beauty in the dusk
darkening sky above garages, western suburbs.
Pale green and melted yellow streak
across the stage of sunset: back porches
up on third and even fourth floor brick walkups.

Sun moon dusk dawn – we have them in the city.
Stars fall from the urban sky, land on solid ground:
sidewalks sparkle diamond mica jewels
under our shoes, concrete silica glitter shines
for moon, for sun, for mercury vapor lamps.

Grasses grow along the tracks, bending low to wind.
Commuter trains race Queen Anne's lace. Milkweed
and wild rye live here in the city, where silver rails –
one, two and the deadly third, speed our fast riding
passing trees: night and morning, night and morning.

City River

Does the river know it once was wild?
Forced against itself, drawn away from the great lake
can the water live in its memory of stones rounded smooth
trees leaning over glassy pools, great birds
hovering diving striking at the flash of silver in rocky shallows?

Does the river remember it could be *heard*
riffling, booming, churning down its length to the lake?
Can it remember that once, long time gone
before this oily green, its water ran shining, breathing
black with clean mud, running clear beyond the marsh?

Does it see people in fatbottomed tourboats
rows of metal chairs on deck, loud: "...the Merchandise
Mart, owned at one time by Joseph Kennedy...."? Can the river
recall the others, those who silently rode its living surface
rippling beneath their painted boats?

Does the river sometimes wonder if those people
took the trees, dropped the stones into their leather packs
and walked away? Or can the river know that they too
long time gone, lost the sky, the birds, the bright flashing fish
and thick banks of dark earth, dense with roots?

The Crows

Middle-aged women are flocking to see the crows.
They stand on sidewalks, on lawns, and they stare
at the tops of telephone poles, the highest branches
of trees; they sit on picnic tables in the park, perch
at the fountain's edge to watch the crows walk
slowly through strips of sunlight between trees
their black eyes sharp as scissors, knives, razors
black feathers brightly purpled by the light, satin
green and blue, shocking streaks of sudden red
shining off the blackest backs of crows who never
look at the women, crows who walk, stop, open
wide capes of wing and flex their black stick legs
to enter the air. They rise to fly, calling each other
by name, calling each other's names out of the sky.

All That We Do Here

The first snow of winter is shining across the sidewalks
making us think of what comes last, after this
glory of flakes swirling, glittering past streetlights
sweeping through shadowy canyons downtown
freezing us in winter's glamour. We know all that
we do here, what we have done here, covering
ground with our streets, will cover the snow.

What the Birds Say

... the birds bring messages from the dead, and the dead
bring messages from the universe. - *Susan Griffin*

That year I lived in Chicago again, back home
by the lake, but getting ready to leave.
I was thinking of the past when they died;
birds came every day, flying me into the future.

I lived with the birds; we nested almost together
up on the third floor corner. They coveted my porch
and my kitchen, flapped into my neighbor's fenced trees.
I envied their sky. I watched their wings.

Winter pigeons huddled at my leaded panes
burbling city secrets in their breasts;
gulls flew seventeen blocks in the spring
to my porch, shrieking *lake, beach,* all over my desk.

The summer birds, sparrows in cherry trees
next door, were louder than light in the morning;
Canada geese came by in the fall, flapping
to Rosehill, walking in grass all over the dead.

Crows fly there round the year, flocking
the graveyard trees. They croak
the raw call of their shiny black throats;
they perch on the gravestones and scream.

No one of mine was there in the ground
but four were dying that year every day
while I walked through Rosehill crying
reading aloud the stones of strangers.

I walked with the birds in Rosehill, listening
thinking of dying, what I would lose and how
it would go for me, after. I waited for messages.
What do they say? I asked each time, What?

I asked them all. The raucous gulls laughed at me.
The pigeons said, We don't care. The sparrows were
so loud they never heard me and the geese flew south
rising on wings spread like blankets all over my head.

I went to the crows. In the garden of dead people
I cried to them each time: Where have they gone?
Tell me. They must have words for me, give me
their words. They want me to know. Tell me.

The crows flicked their little black eyes; they looked at me.
They pecked in the grass and made crackling sounds.
I went home and packed up the dishes, folded
my clothes, and put tape around all of the boxes.

Soon

I go to the woods to write
and the phone rings there
where I sit among the cousins
of telephone poles, their mothers
aunts and uncles, fathers still
rooted and deeply breathing –
the phone rings, and I answer
from my chair in a room of glass
tall windows gleaming into green
leaves and needles waving
in a rising wind, gesturing
to each other here in the woods
where, oddly, the phone rings.

My father is dying. I know
he's been slowly loosening
connections, his breath so quiet
I strain to hear it; all of him
slower and getting smaller
even the slight smile at his own
impatient preference for shade –
now he's picking up speed
like the forest breeze, soft still
but swiftening, using up time
faster than flying a thousand miles:
leaves is suddenly a verb
needles are surgical steel.

Lately when I called he'd say: See?
Dial this number, you still get me.
Today you did, soon you won't.
He laughs and coughs a little.
Soon I'll be in his room, gone
from these windows
made of light; I'll be gone
from trees made of light
by science and magic –
to sit in the dark by his bed
where he says no, no, don't
open the curtains; it's too much.
I don't want the light.

After years of graceful branches

At the end of one week, this wild river is fast
and loud; trees have become our familiars; light rushes over
morning's stones, darkening past the island

One of us writes, another stops, three read
where the wide porch floor is softening with dropped needles
the moving air is cool and the high sun is hot

While we work, the river streams through words
and trees crowd onto our notebooks; fallen rocks, silken moss
cracked branches write themselves into our pages

Here, where riverlight streaks past the porch
we study together, seeded by chance like cedar and hemlock
rising up out of the ground beside this river

How many of each grow in that deep stand?
we see ruddy cedar's dense green, shag of layered bark so heavy
those hemlocks are obscured, hardly visible

Until the bright gleam off the river shifts
grey shadows cross a thicket, making the cedar's rough trunk
disappear from sight: hemlock emerges

Looking away when the sun moves through
curly ferns dripping at river's edge – then looking back again
changes the scene: you see only hemlock

Surely one lesson where such trees grow together
(into lumber, pulp, tannic acid after years of graceful branches)
must be learning how to see that moving light

This Side of the River

When the rain wind comes, green leaves turn over greysilver
but that tree, there, who can say why or how it happens
that one's leaves turn gold – over there, across the river, see?

Now blue is not only for berries, for tipping delphinium stalks.
That big spruce on the hill reflects the northwest sky, greyblue
as if dusted, beyond deciduous green, singular among firs.

Which of them might have the knowledge of good and evil?
Which is the tree of life? And is there a tree of death, iron hard
tall beside an underground throne that has no need of shade?

If we eat of its fruit, we become *like gods* – is that good? Evil?
And what are they *like*, *gods*? Do we know? Do we desire
what most of us find only in translation, in paraphrase?

Do you understand the languages of trees? Most of us can't
ask them these questions; we can only raise our eyes, worship
their solemnity, their reach, their rough skin made of rain.

The Man Who Loves Trees

loves through the seasons:
bare trunk, fat buds, full green, wet red
and their names: sweet gum
cypress oak spruce willow maple
red bud forest pansy
and their parts: leaf cone flower
bark root branch boll twig needle
lacy fans of rough crochet, pods
like cigars, like rattling gourds.

He loves their cast-offs crisp on the ground
their sound under his boots on the trail
rustling, breaking down into dust.
He loves, later, their sawn boards:
wood, its grain a watery maze
polished, rubbed into light, glowing
still with heat from the heart of the tree
like his own heart, pumping dark liquid
out to the limbs, out to his own warm hands.

Birth Days

Every forest remembers its own green birth in dirt.

I remember sun on my skin that summer: heat and light.
Like trees, we two were seeded by wind and rain.

The moon was red or silver, the waves were black or gold.
We walked the shore of the lake through night to morning.

Every forest loses trees to lightning, clean and dead.
Then tight green curls push out, up through hard black sand.

We were struck over and over, toppled, emptied and scoured.

Learning from that flash of sudden fire, we saw by sky light
what's born inside of flame, what lives inside of coal.

Here From Somewhere Else

Sometimes the market band
(here from somewhere else)
plays bluegrass.

The grass looks green, tree
green in the sun, goes blue
in shade, low-flying shadows.

Every night (the band says)
dusk leans over Kentucky:
long meadows, tall grass
bowing, shading itself blue.

Every morning, dew slides
slender light along grass
blades, bending them blue.

The slide, the bend and bowing –
they're all here, in delicate boxes:
banjo, mandolin, fiddle & guitar.

The mouth harp blues them down.

Metamorphoses

I may have become the old woman
   who lives in a cottage deep in the woods.

I might be the wolf who meets a child coming to visit
   carrying her basket of bread and jam for Granny.

Perhaps I'm a wicked stepmother urging her man to abandon
   his children – or the shallow, careless father who does.

I could be one of the thickly branching oaks, a rough pebble
   among their roots – a mossy stone, or a beetle climbing over it.

What if I were an ivory owl, swooping at those cheeky squirrels
   taking one while the others scatter in terror of my wings?

No reason not to be a fox, clever and plush, or a mushroom
   rising silently out of the dense bracken.

Even the dark bird who watches from the top of the tall aspen
   when children leave home wearing mittens and scarves.

I see those children waiting for the yellow bus.
   They have no idea.

Wild River Sister

Her bright hair is shining
flying over her mind
flying like river spray
like the white haired river –
green-blue water body
startling as turquoise
stones from the desert
gone loose, filled with light
running liquid, rushing
west over the land, west
to this cold water, thrashing
its white hair, racing
its own foam down a chute
between rocks – the river is
churning, like her mind.

Light Falling Here

(always, writers say, the light on the water
shines like diamonds, shines like gold
but the truth is that gold, and that diamonds
want only to shine like the light on the water)

Just now, on the early morning river
every spangle is a bird
flashing tiny wings of light;
the sun has thrown a sheet of hammered gold
over the slow skin of the dawn river;
a raft of light turns on dark water
tethered to the boat dock
moving with the river.

And I, waking here,
dreamed the sun falling down in the ocean
light in the heart of the sea
fire at the heart of the sea
my heart is on fire in the water
light burns in the heart of the sea
seawater skin on the body of sunset
sunset a fire at the watery edge of the world
fire all there at the edge of the world
burning the skin of the water
wet sand a mirror for fire in the water
sunset a tipped bowl of flame
I ask myself, again

Can I be in love with the light on the water? so in love that
I long for that light on the top of a mountain
and in the prairie need to touch it with my eyes?
In forest the light comes pouring all down, gilding a pool
where sun finds a break in the trees and I, mouth open
lips burning, kneel blinded inside the blaze.
I yearn for the liquid full moon, running silk silver all night
crave lightning on through the wash of the rain
weep at stars that tip waves in the lake.
I want to see fireclouds up in the sky
their waterhearts pierced by the sun
to drown through geometry gleaming in light
on the floor of a sunstruck pond.

Now again sun falls into ocean, moon rises out in far sky
they stream to me, here on the shore
light shivers the water, goldsilver crosses the sky
crosses the world, this whole world coming to me
the shivering glimmering path leads to me
just here to my face, to my feet
moons and suns rising and falling in water
light falling here into love.

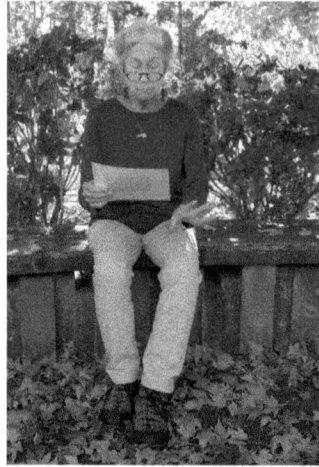

About the Author

Born and raised in the Great Lakes region, Judith Arcana has lived in the Pacific Northwest since 1995. She writes poems, stories, essays and books, including a well-loved biography of Grace Paley (*Grace Paley's Life Stories*), the poetry collections *What if your mother*, *4th Period English*, *The Parachute Jump Effect* and *The Water Portfolio*, a set of three lyric broadsides. Her story *Soon To Be A Major Motion Picture* won the first Minerva Rising Prose Prize and was published as a chapbook; *Keesha and Joanie and JANE,* her zine about what happens when Roe v Wade is overturned in the near future, is rooted in her work as a Jane in Chicago's underground abortion service (Judith has written a collection of Jane stories and hopes to see the book published in 2016). Visit juditharcana.com for more about – and examples of – her work.

www.ingramcontent.com/pod-product-compliance
Lightning Source LLC
Chambersburg PA
CBHW032109040426
42449CB00007B/1233